BEARS TO CARVE

with
Dale Power

Text written with and photography by Jeffrey B. Snyder

Schiffer
Publishing Ltd

77 Lower Valley Road, Atglen, PA 19310

Contents

Copyright © 1995 by Dale Power.
Library of Congress Cataloging-in-Publication Data
Power, Dale.
    Bears to Carve with Dale Power/text written with
  and photography by Jeffrey B. Snyder.
     p. cm.
  ISBN 0-88740-719-6
  1. Wood-carving. 2. Wood-carved figurines. 3. Polar bear in art.
  4. Bears in art. I. Snyder, Jeffrey B. II. Title
TT199.7.P69 1995
731'.832–dc20
                           94-23248
                              CIP

Printed in China.
ISBN: 0-88740-719-6

Published by Schiffer Publishing, Ltd.
77 Lower Valley Road
Atglen, PA 19310
Please write for a free catalog.
This book may be purchased from the publisher.
Please include $2.95 postage.
Try your bookstore first.

We are interested in hearing from authors
with book ideas on related subjects.

Introduction

The polar bear conjures up images of long cold winters in Alaska. One of my favorite scenes is of a polar bear belly down on the ice at a fishing hole. He covers his dark nose with his great white paw, fooling an unsuspecting seal into dropping in for dinner. Many of my students love the ease of carving this wonderful beast. As you follow the instructions in this book, I hope you will agree with them.

Bears have been great favorites in zoos for hundreds of years. Their great strength is impressive and the sheer size of some bears is enough to gain instant respect. If you look close when a bear is standing up on it's hind feet, you will see it looks remarkably like a giant person.

Male bears are called boars and females are called sows. Young bears are called cubs, of course. Sows are usually smaller than boars and, as a rule, they avoid the larger males. Only during mating season do sows and boars spend time together.

Of all the large meat eating animals, some of the bears are among the largest. A sizable tiger may weigh about 770 pounds but a big bear can weigh three times as much. For years the Kodiak brown bear was called the biggest bear alive; however, in 1962, a polar bear that was more than eleven feet tall, weighed in at an incredible 2,210 pounds.

Like humans, bears (with five toes on each foot) put their feet down flat on the ground when they walk. Most other large animals (dogs, horses, even elephants) walk on their toes. Unlike humans, bears can run as fast as a horse for brief distances on their short, powerful legs.

Despite their size, polar bears are graceful and athletic. They jump over cracks in the ice more than 20 feet wide. They are also expert long distance swimmers.

Polar bears look like other bears except for a few obvious differences. Their heads are narrower and their ears are smaller. They also have white fur.

Once fully grown, a polar bear is safe from almost anything except other bears and humans. If they escape these dangers, polar bears may live as long as forty years.

My polar bear is carved out of Basswood, also known as American Linden, because of the forgiving nature of the wood as well as the high quality and durability of the final product. It is classified as a hardwood, but I find it great for either hand or machine carving.

While we're speaking of carving, I use a bench knife, a set of assorted hand gouges, an Automat Power Chisel, a Detail Master Wood Burning System, a Foredom flexible shaft machine, and an Optima-2 high speed grinder. Both the Foredom and the Optima-2 are fitted with assorted carbide burrs for this project. The paints are acrylic washes.

Whenever you use sharp tools, a Kevlar woodcarver's glove is a wise choice to protect your hand from the blades. **However, it is important to remember NEVER to use the glove while using rotary power tools. The potential for getting the burr wrapped in the glove, causing serious personal injury, is simply too great.**

It is always wise to protect your lungs with a dust mask or a dust collection system when you use power tools. Thus prepared, I hope you will enjoy the book and have as much fun carving your polar bear as I've had carving mine.

Carving the Bear

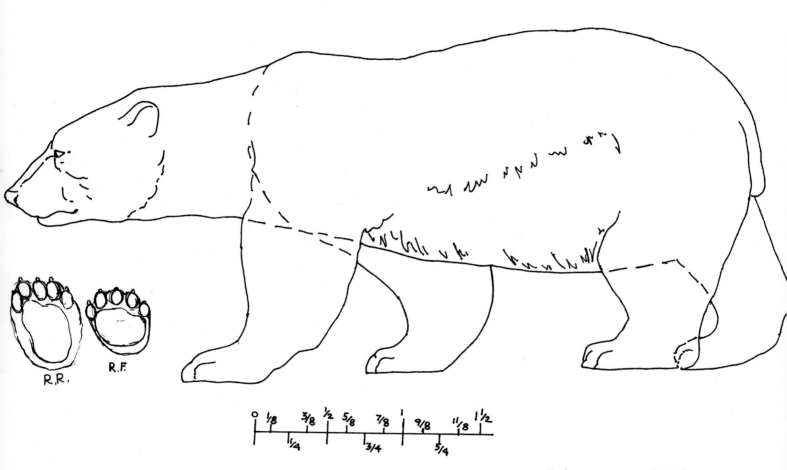

R.R.   R.F.

0 1/8 3/8 1/2 5/8 7/8 1 9/8 11/8 1 1/2
       1/4   3/4   5/4

*Enlarge pattern 152%
for original size.*

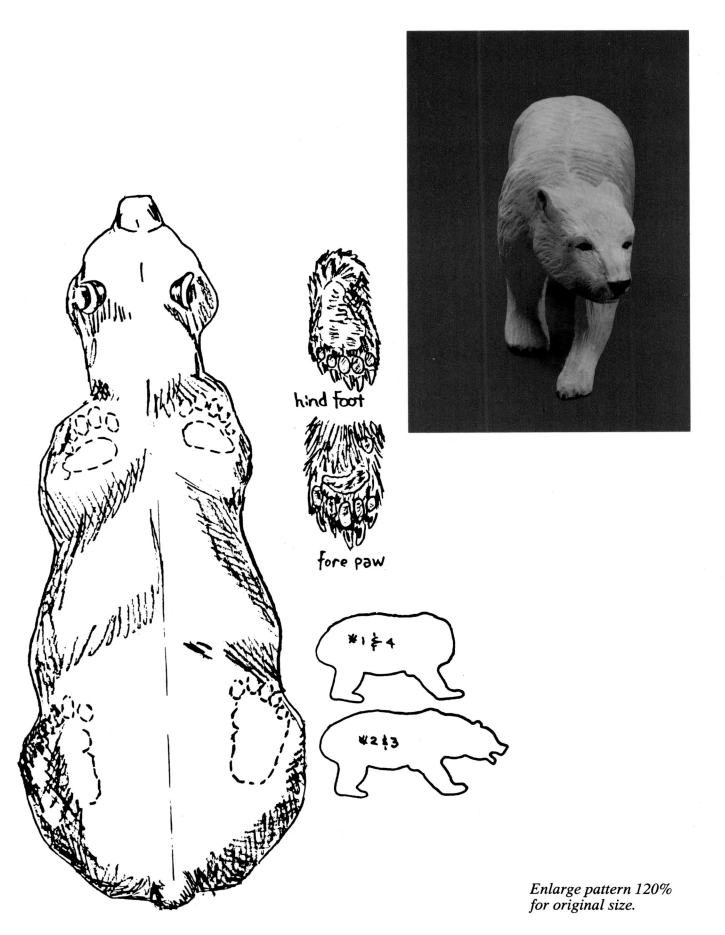

hind foot

fore paw

#1 & 4

#2 & 3

*Enlarge pattern 120%
for original size.*

5

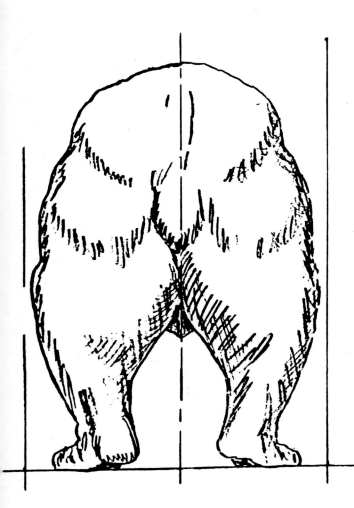
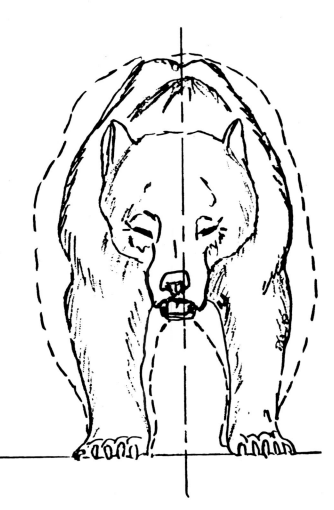

Enlarge pattern 120% for original size.

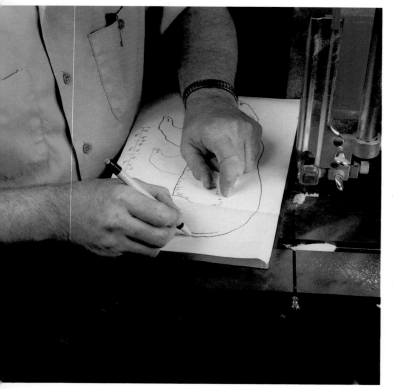

The polar bear, also known as the white bear, is the largest of the known carnivores. The largest polar bear on record weighs 2,210 pounds and stands eleven feet high on his back legs. Quite well adapted to the arctic regions, the polar bear's head and ears are small. It's back is slightly arched. Although the bear's fur is pure white, the skin is black and shows on the tip of his nose and around his lips. The eyes are small and dark, with little expression. The feet are heavily furred and the polar bear walks in a pigeon-toed gait. My bear is laid out on 1" x 7" basswood. You will need enough wood to reproduce the individual pieces of the bear four times. First, use carbon paper to trace the pattern onto the wood.

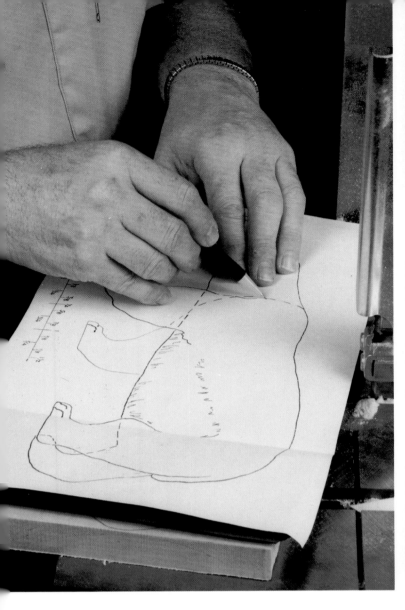

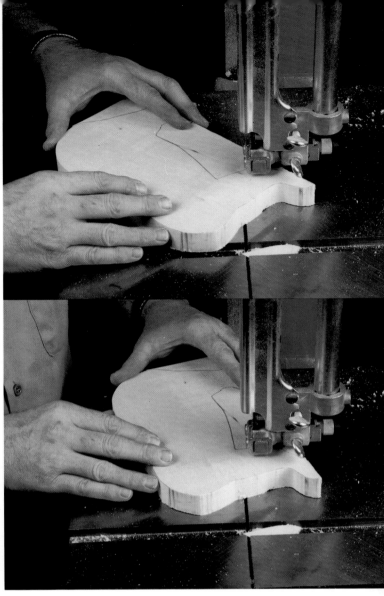

These dotted lines indicate where one of the outside pieces will be cut off.

This is one of the outside pieces with the shoulder exposed. Note the lack of a head on this piece as you remove the excess stock.

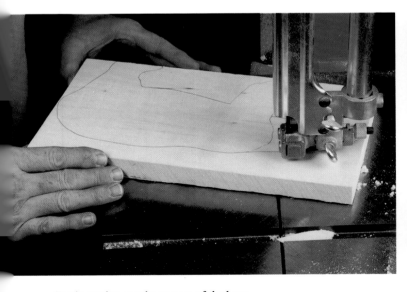

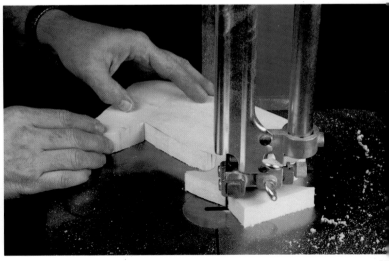

Begin cutting out the pattern of the bear.

Here is how the outside piece should look once the excess stock has been removed.

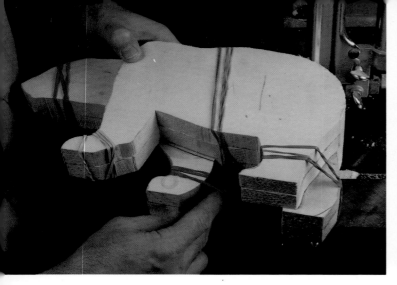

Glue all of the pieces together with yellow carpenter's glue, placing as many clamps as you have on the pieces. If you do not have clamps, heavy rubber bands will do an adequate job.

After the glue has cured for about twelve hours, remove the rubber bands and draw on a center line where the two inside pieces meet.

The measurements for laying out the bear are based on the total length of the bear's head. The scale at the bottom of the drawing will allow you to keep the dorsal view of the bear in proper dimension.

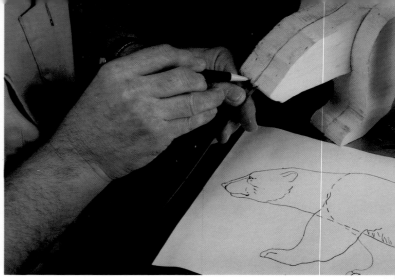

The bear's nose is one quarter the total length of the head.

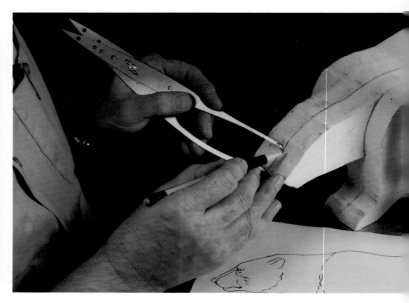

The length of the nose is one half of the total length of the head ...

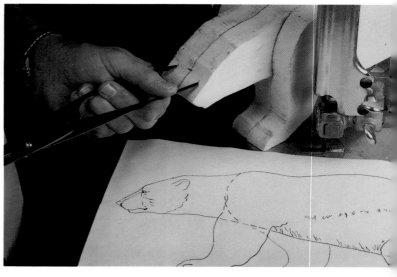

... and the width of the bear's nose is also one half of the total length of the head.

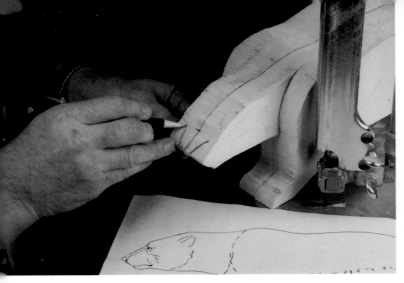

Connect the dots as you go. Here is the nose.

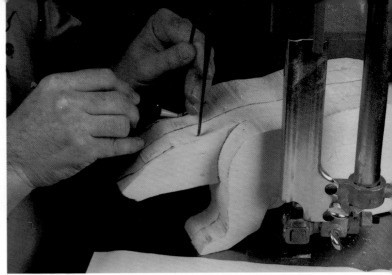

Half way down the length of the neck, the measurement will be 5/8 of the head's total length.

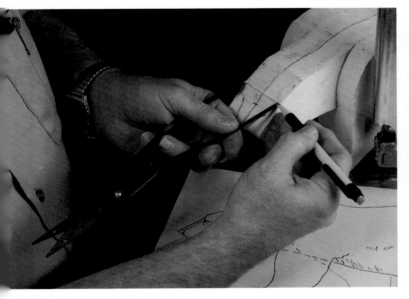

The width of the bear's head across the forehead is 5/8 of the total length of his head.

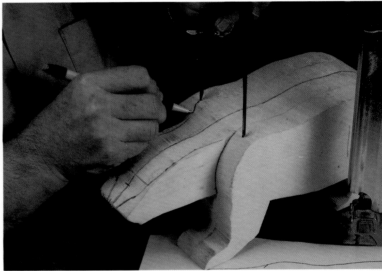

The width at the shoulders will be 1 3/8 times the total length of the head.

At the point where the ears will be carved in, the width of the wood will measure 3/4 of the total length of the head.

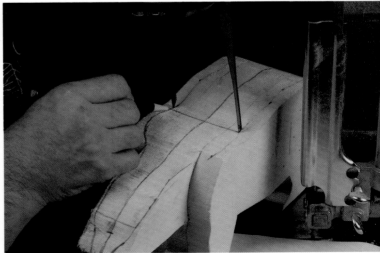

The area between the shoulders and the belly will be 1 1/8 the head's total length.

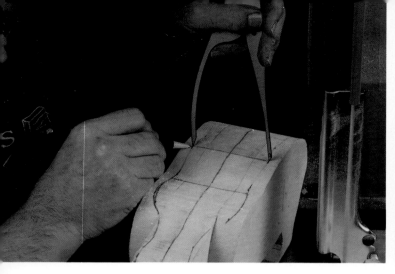

The measurement through the thickest part of the stomach is 1 3/8 the total length of the head.

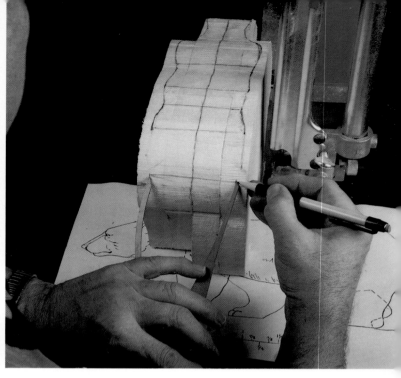

The last measurement at the root of the tail is 1 1/4 the total length of the head.

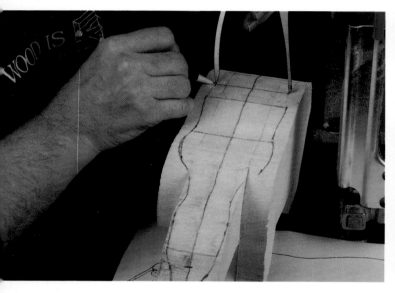

The next measurement is where the stomach dips in, just in front of the flanks, 1 1/8 the total length of the head.

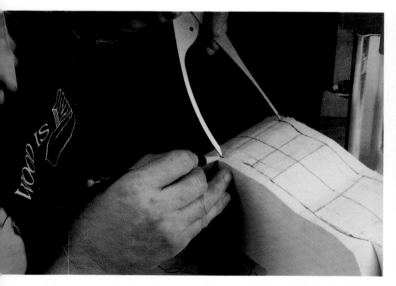

Next measure the broadest part of the rear flanks, 1 3/8 the head's total length.

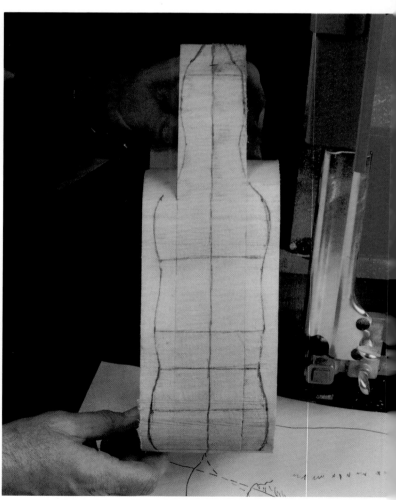

When you have completed drawing on the dorsal view, connecting all the dots, it should appears something like this.

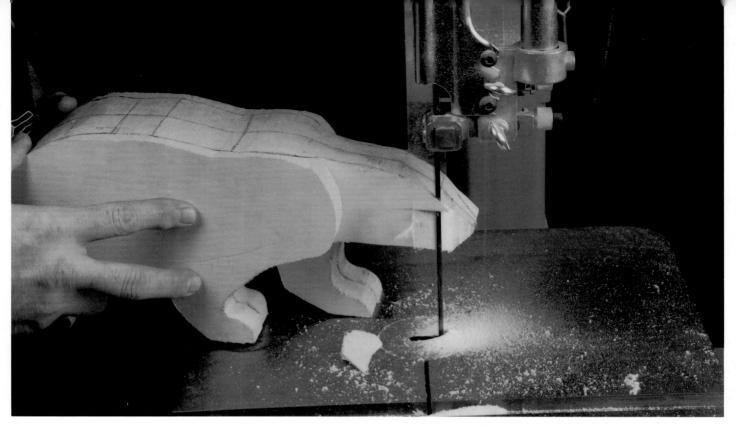

Now we are going to cut out the dorsal view with the band saw. While using the saw do not place your fingers under the bear, through the legs, as this may well result in injury to your fingers. Begin cutting out the dorsal view, following the guide lines you have just completed. This takes away some of the waste wood and speeds the carving.

Continue cutting out the dorsal view.

Use a little piece of wood to push the bear through and protect your fingers from the blade.

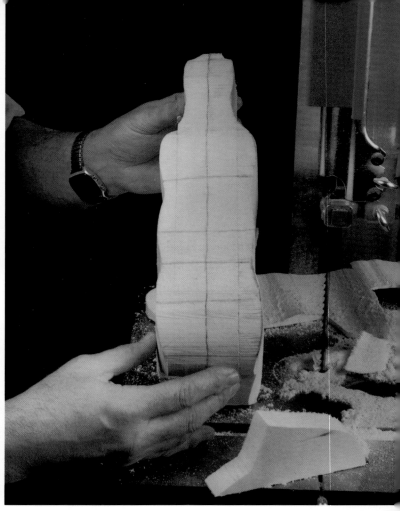

One completed side of the dorsal view. The excess falls away.

With the dorsal view completely cut out, we are ready to either begin carving or, as an option, to cut the head off to turn it.

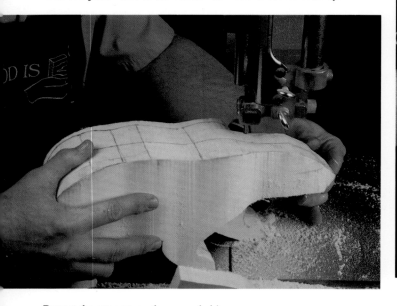

Repeat the process on the second side.

Let's turn the head. Draw a line on the neck at an angle of approximately 30 degrees or less.

Now draw a straight line indicating the square cut.

Make a square cut to remove the bear's head.

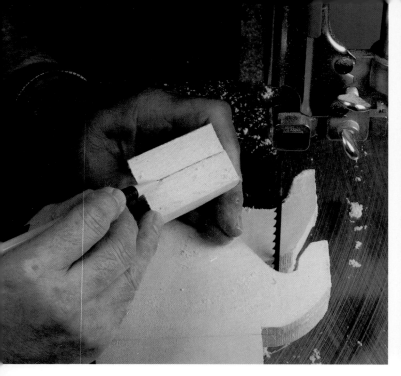

Draw in the center line on the cut portion of the neck to provide a guide to replace the head squarely on the bear.

If you are using a band saw, tilt your table to 30 degrees. Lay the bear on its side and follow the top edge of the neck as a guide to keep your cut straight.

The angle has been removed.

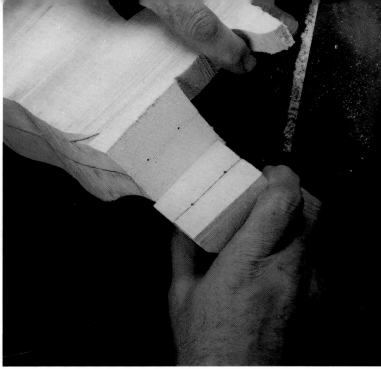

Prepared to turn the bear's head, we now use small brads inserted into the head portion of the bear's neck to mark the locations where we need to drill holes in the portion of the neck attached to the body of the bear. Cut the heads off the brads and place them in the head portion of the bear's neck, following the center line.

The brads are in place.

Remove the brads. The guide holes are in place. Enlarge the holes with your drill, using a 1/8" drill bit.

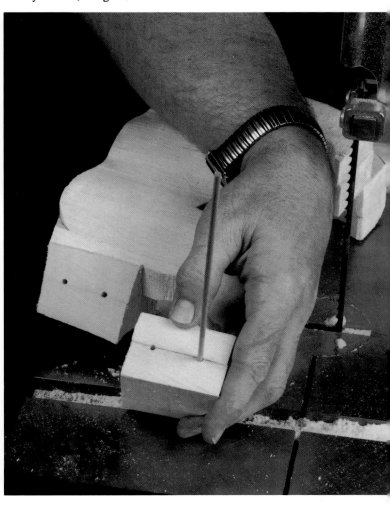

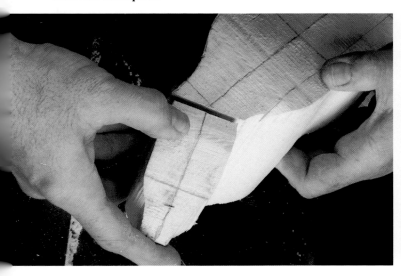

Line up the center lines and force the head in place. The brads mark the places where holes are to be drilled.

Insert a 1/8 inch wooden dowel into each hole in the head, gluing the dowels in place with yellow carpenter's glue.

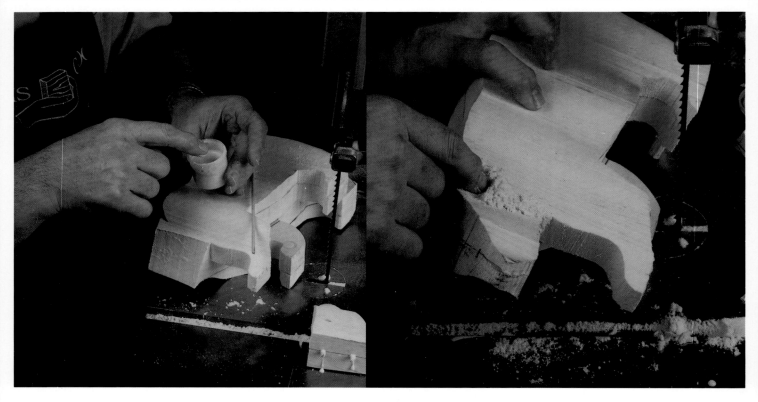

Spread a thin layer of yellow carpenter's glue on the joint.

Pack the sawdust and glue liberally into the joint.

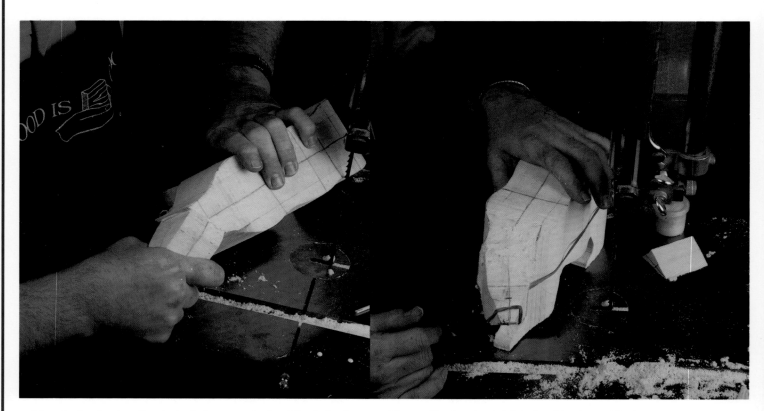

After placing the doweling in the holes, press the head firmly in place. Any gaps that appear may be compensated for at this time with a mixture of sawdust and yellow carpenter's glue.

Use a rubber band to hold the head in place while the glue dries. Now set the bear aside, allowing the glue to cure for about 12 hours.

To start rounding off the polar bear, first lay out the side view. The dorsal view has already been cut out.

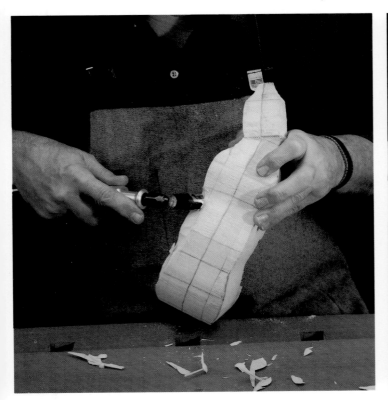

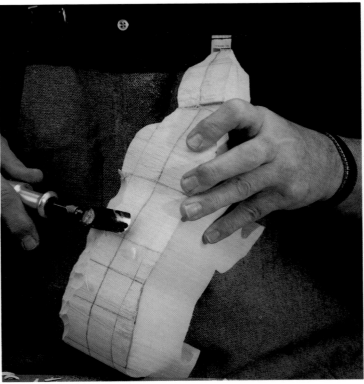

Starting with the largest chisel you can put in your Automat Wood Carving Power Chisel, begin to round off the polar bear. This powered chisel speeds up the rounding process. You may use hand-held chisels to do the same job, but the powered chisel makes rounding a little more enjoyable. Begin with the top edge, rounding toward the center line.

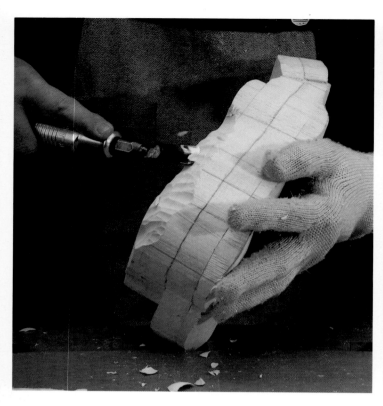

Continue rounding down. I suggest you use a Kevlar safety glove as it will lessen the chance of injury. The cost of the glove is considerably less than an expensive trip to the emergency room for stitches. These gloves are usually available through any carving supply house.

We will only be rounding down about 1/3 of the way on both sides to define two upper muscle patterns on the sides of the polar bear. This is about as far as you need to go.

The rounded sides; note that the area of the tail is left unrounded.

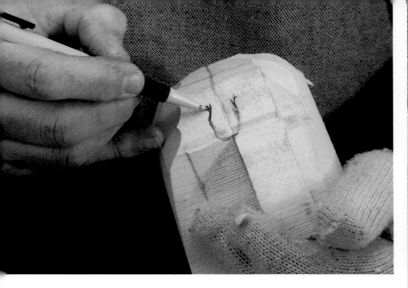

The tail of a polar bear is very small. Draw in the area of that small tail now.

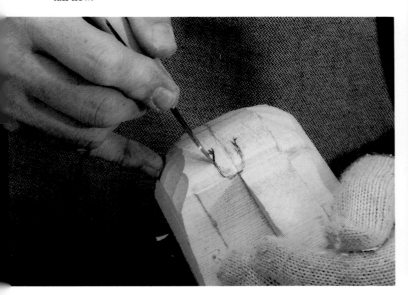

Make a stop cut with a bench knife around the tail.

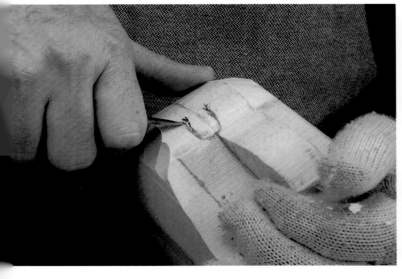

Now relieve the area of wood around the stop cut so you won't cut away the tail with your powered chisel.

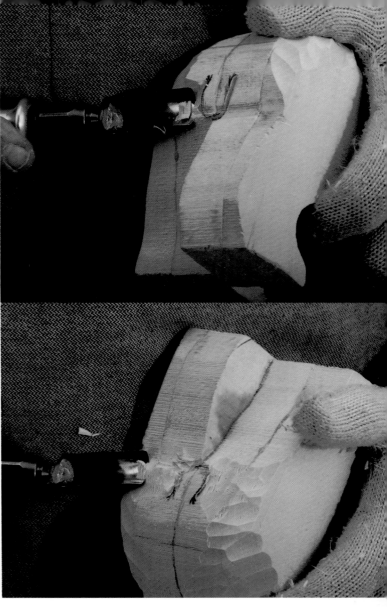

Remove the excess wood, exposing the bear's tail in preparation to carving the back legs.

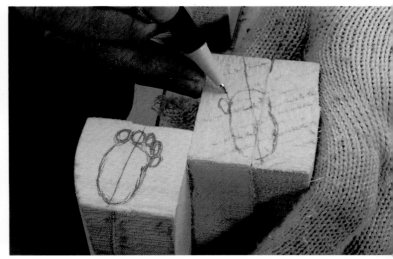

Polar bears walk pigeon-toed, so we want to indicate the angle of this bear's feet and draw them in as shown here.

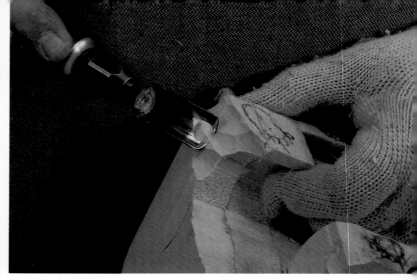

Continue rounding down the feet.

Here are the four pigeon-toed feet. Now you have defined an area to carve down to for the feet.

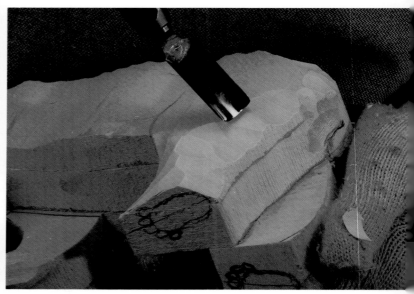

Go ahead, round up the back legs as well.

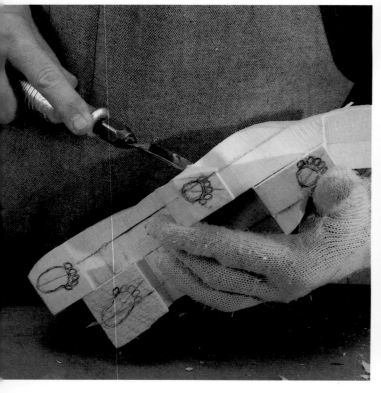

Begin taking off the excess wood around the feet.

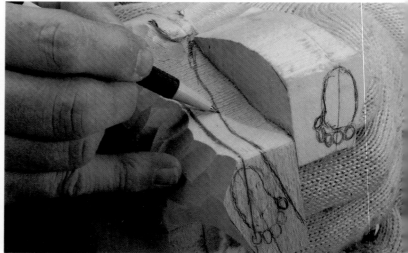

In a gentle arc from a point just below his tail down to the outside edge of his toes, draw a line to indicate the area between the rear legs which is to be removed. Repeat for both legs.

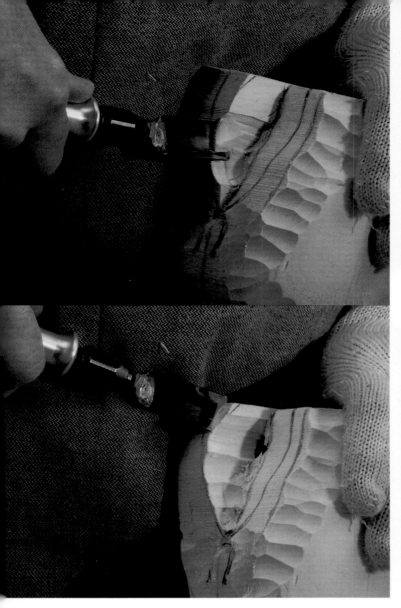

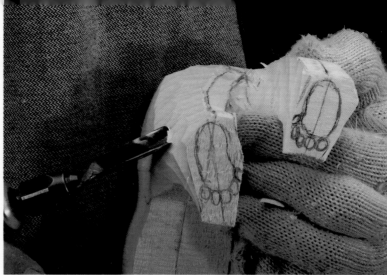

Tapering to the point on the back leg.

Remove the excess wood from between the rear legs with the powered chisel.

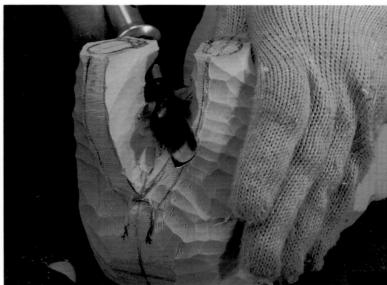

Taper both the inside and outside of each back leg to the central point along the rear of each leg.

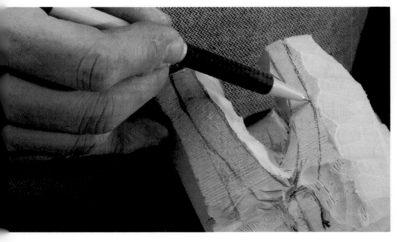

Here is how the rounded rear legs should look with the excess wood removed from between them. Also, note that on the back of the legs the hair tapers from both sides to a central point. Draw in a center line as a guide when tapering to this point.

Here is how the tapered rear legs should look.

21

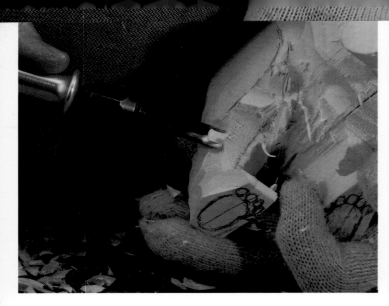

Round the lower part of the rear leg.

Here's how the insides of the rear legs should look when they are rounded.

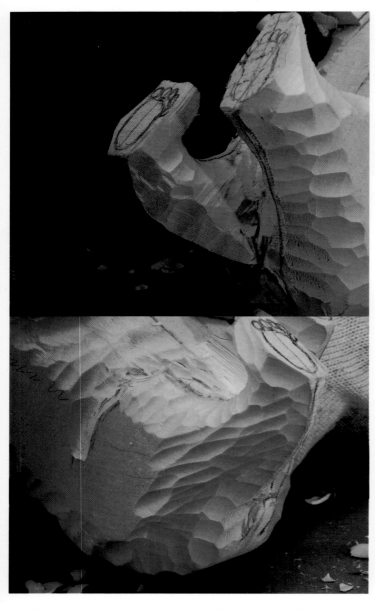

Here is how the rounded rear leg should look. Repeat this process for the other rear leg.

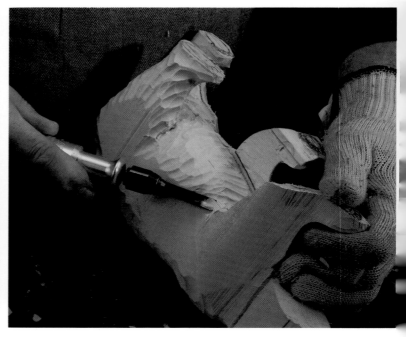

Continue rounding the belly up to the front legs.

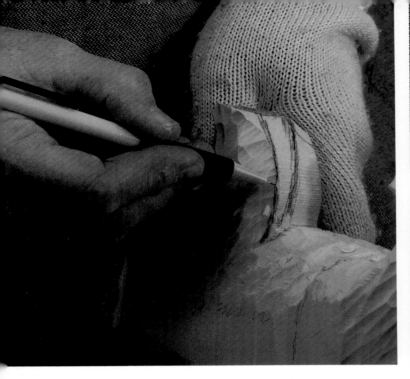

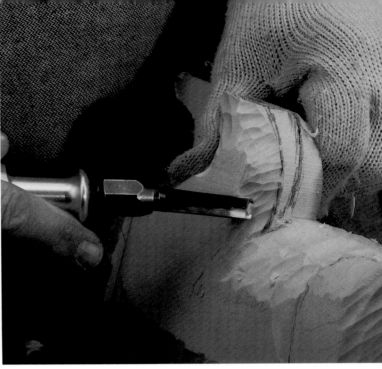

Round the rear outside edge of the trailing front leg to a line that begins at the center of the foot and arcs outward to the outside edge of the body.

Rounding to this arcing line.

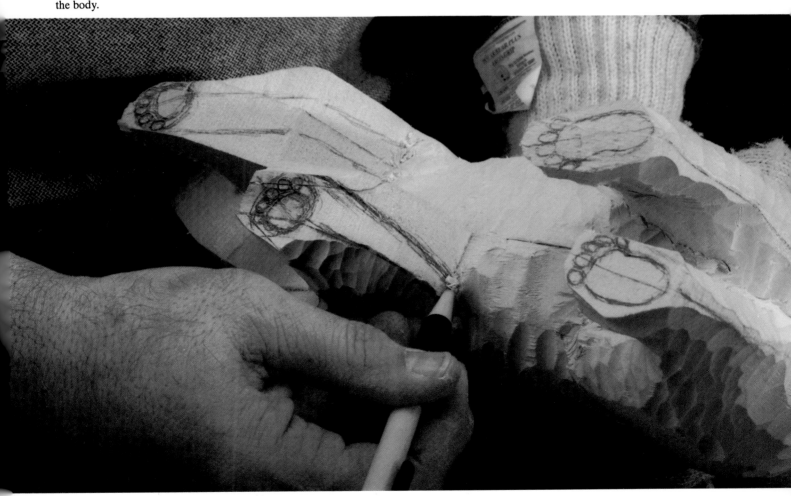

Indicate the inside of the front leg from the edge of the foot to a point 1/4 of an inch thick where it touches the body.

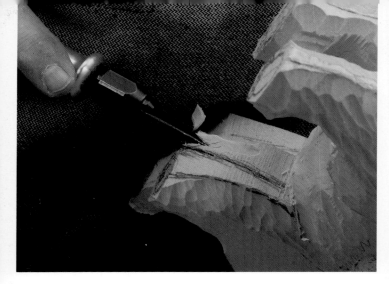

Remove the excess wood.

Round down the outside of the leading front leg to the rear center line in the same manner as before.

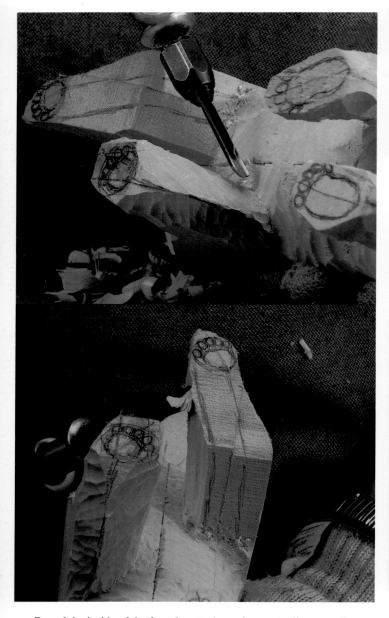

Round the inside of the front legs to the arcing center line as well.

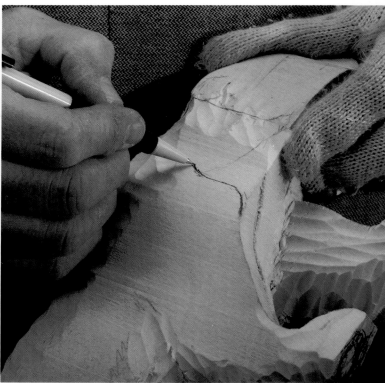

Indicate the leading edge of the front shoulder on the right side of the bear.

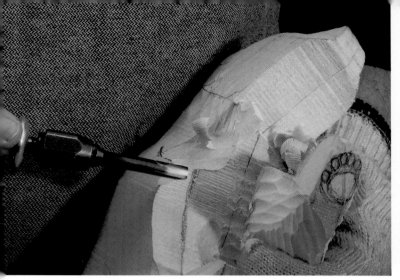

Cut out in front of the shoulder to indicate the muscles of the neck.

Begin rounding to the center line on the front leg.

Continue removing wood from the area of the neck.

Here is how the rounded outside of the front leg should look.

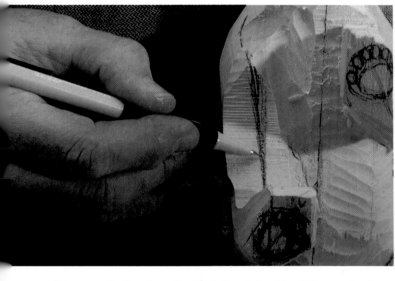

Draw a center line down the front of each front leg. We are going to round to it.

Rounding down the inside of the front leg to the center line.

Here is the completely rounded front leg.

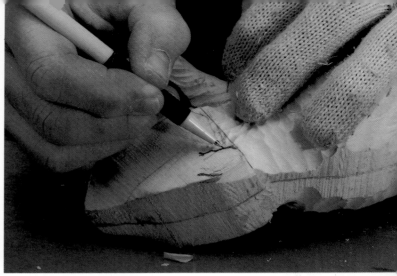

Now rough in the location of the ears on the head so that you will remember to leave enough wood to carve them later.

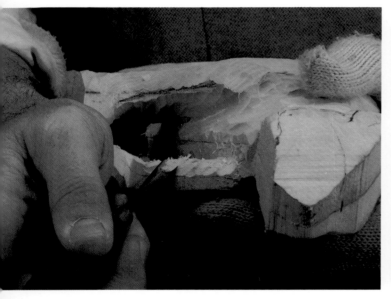

Switch to a small 1/4" gouge chisel to clean out small areas that are hard to reach with a larger tool. Here we are working on the left front leg.

We're going to define the muscles in the neck, working from the back of the jaw toward the shoulder.

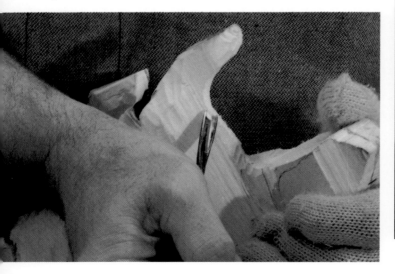

Shaping the outside of the right front leg.

For defining the muscle that lays in behind the front shoulder at the top of the rib cage, hollowing out underneath the muscle so the bulge above will show that the muscle is there.

Define the division between the front leg and the chest area to create
the illusion that the leg can actually move along the chest.

Now we are going to clean out in front of the rear leg to form a slight
hollow in behind the rib cage. This hollow indicates that the leg has
some place to go as the bear walks.

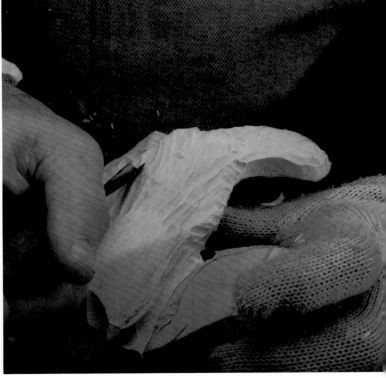

Working on the lower part of the left front leg, we're going to slope the
back of it to the center line, making sure we are not leaving any hard
edges or lines as we work this area down.

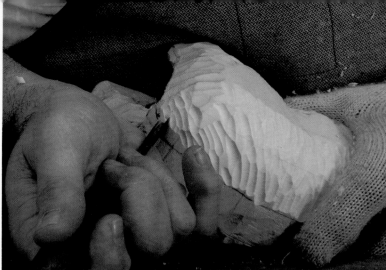

Round the square edges that have been formed by the heavy chisel to start to get a smooth flow from the shoulder to the foot.

Continue shaping over the hind quarters. Repeat the shaping on both sides.

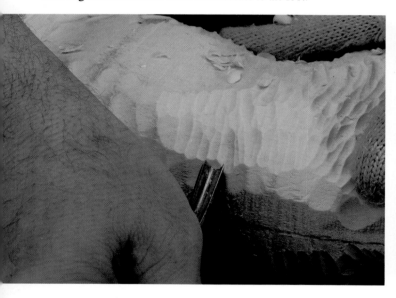

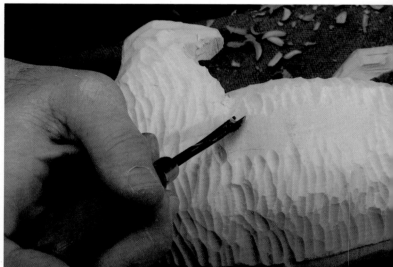

Continue shaping up over the shoulder.

Round down the angular area left on the side of the bear.

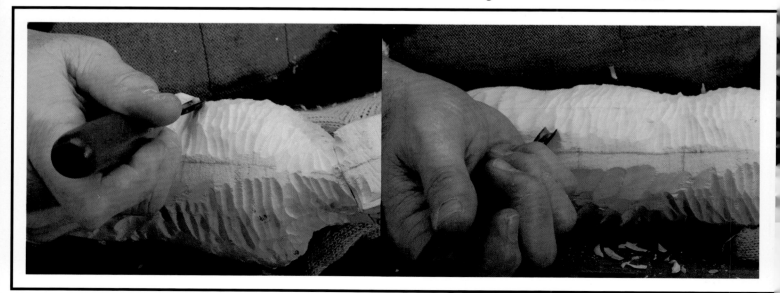

Shaping down the body with the small chisel.

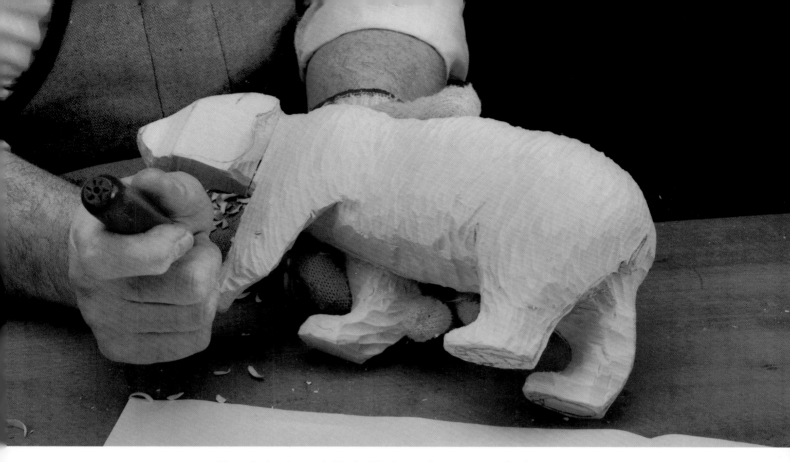

The polar bear's rounded body. Check to make sure you are leaving no flat spots.

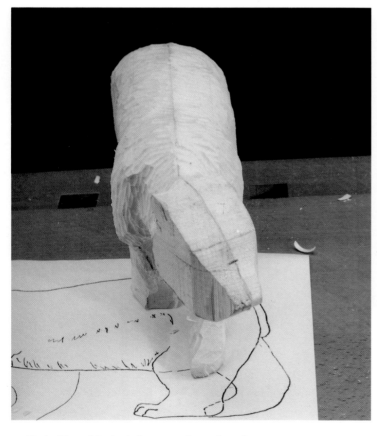

Both sides of the body have now been shaped.

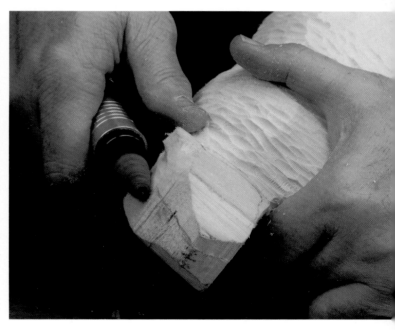

For safety, it is prudent to remove your Kevlar glove at this time as we are switching over to the Foredom flexible shaft machine. Removing the glove eliminates any risk of getting it caught in the rapidly rotating cutting burr attached to the Foredom. Also, for the safety of your lungs, remember to use a dust collector. Now that we have covered the safety tips, in a flexible shaft machine similar to the Foredom I suggest you use the "Christmas tree" shaped Kutzall burr to start shaping the bear's head. The Kutzall quickly and efficiently removes excess wood.

Clean out between the ears to facilitate the flow of the head-neck connection.

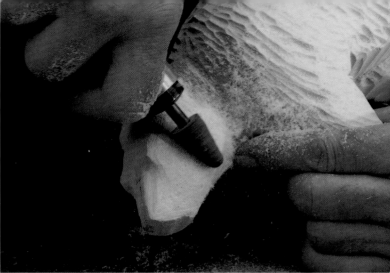

Make sure that the angle from the muzzle to the cheek is a straight line with no humps. Polar bears are swimmers and this smooth line is part of their streamlining.

Round down underneath by the neck.

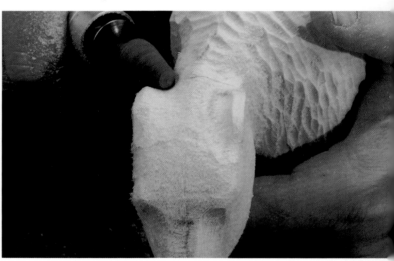

Make sure that you leave plenty of wood for the ears, which will be worked in later. It is important to leave enough wood to prevent the carved ears from becoming thin and fragile. Remember, however, that polar bears do have rather small ears close to the sides of their heads.

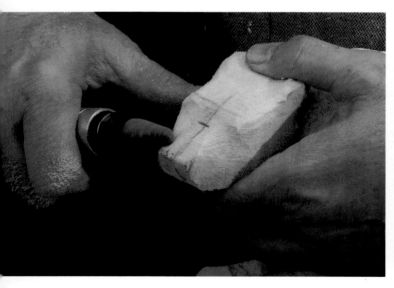

Start to shape the face. Polar bears have pointy, streamlined faces. This shape helps them move speedily through the water, where they spend a large part of their time.

Continuing to use to "Christmas tree" shaped Kutzall, work from the head back along the neck on both sides, smoothing and rounding the muscle masses to indicate the power of the bear.

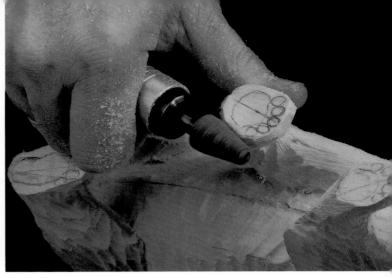

Work back onto the shoulders. There is no large bulge at the shoulders. It is a smooth transition between the shoulder and the neck.

Refer to the drawings you made on the bottoms of the feet to make sure that you don't carve the feet too small. Continue to round all four feet. Remember that the polar bear has a lot of hair covering his feet, even between the toes.

Now remove the excess wood from around the feet.

Round the back, working up onto the sides while making sure to allow the muscle masses to show.

Shape the feet down. Start with the front feet, create a gentle slope from the ankles out to the toes.

Refining an indentation to make the muscle mass show.

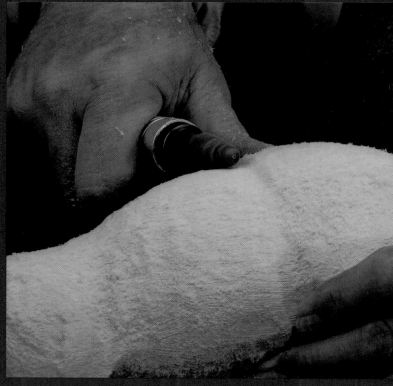

Here is how the rounded side should look. After rounding and shaping one side, making sure the muscle masses show, we'll move to the other side. Starting all over again, work your way from the front shoulder back, making sure that any muscle masses that should show do so at this time.

The large flank muscle is indicated in this area by a groove running back toward the bear's knee.

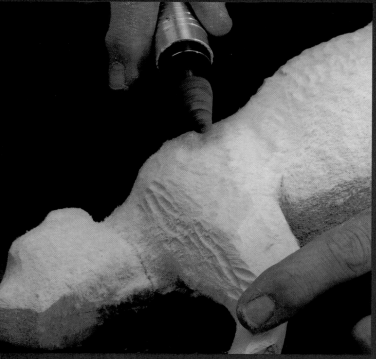

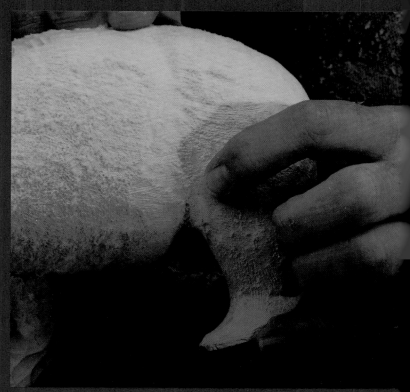

At a point starting just behind the front left shoulder, lay in a small rounded groove that extends out onto the leg, this will indicate the large muscle mass that would be evident with the leg pulled forward in this stance.

The muscle runs from finger tip to finger tip. The bear's knee is located at the lower finger's tip.

Here is the rounded bear.

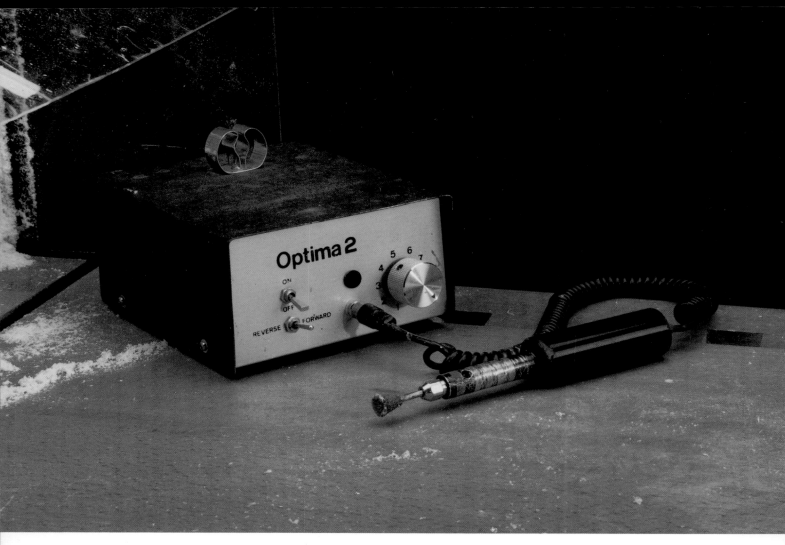

We're going to switch tools now to a small Optima-2 high speed grinder with a reverse-shaped cone to cut the hair into the bear.

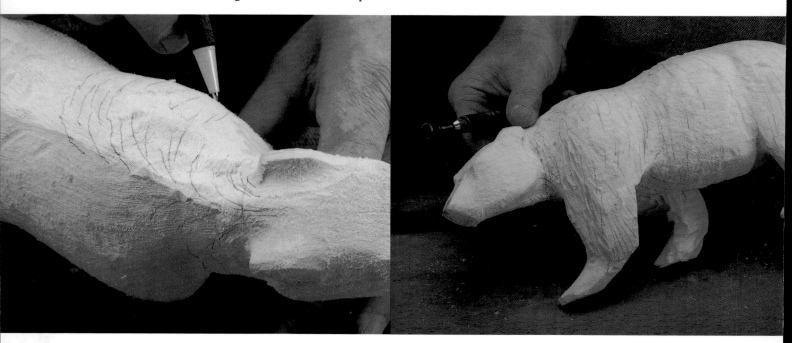

Draw in these lines, indicating the direction that hair flows on the bear.

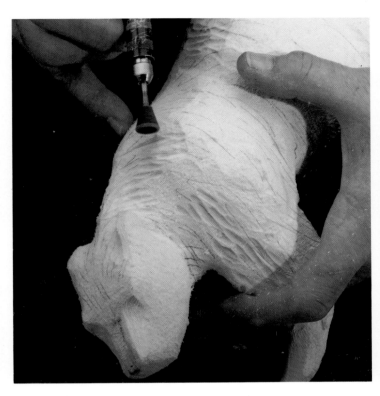

Using the edge of the tool, and making sure you are not cutting absolutely straight lines, you can indicate masses of hair rather than individual hairs. Work from the top of the shoulder back down the sides.

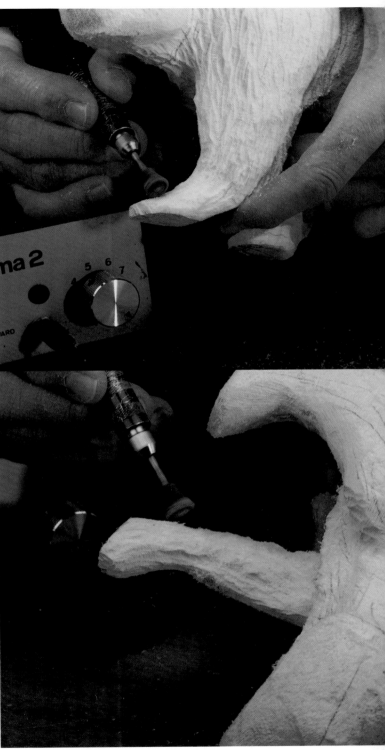

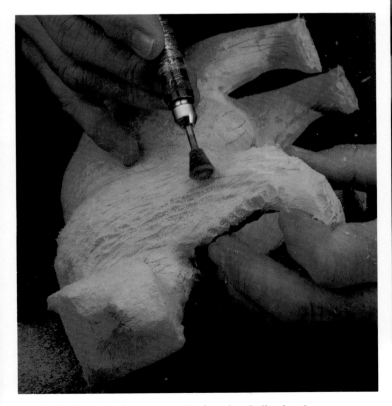

Indicating the hair masses on the front leg. Indicating the masses rather than individual hairs will make the bear seem to have a much fuller and shaggier coat.

When working out on the feet, the strokes become much shorter and tighter together.

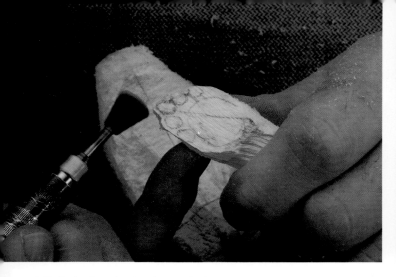

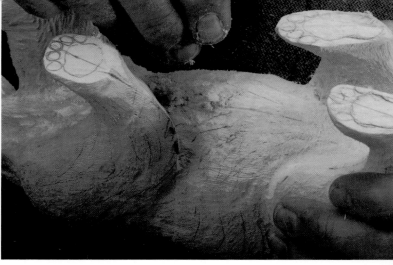

Refer back to the drawing on the bottom of the feet to see where the toes are located. We will now put in the toes with the edge of the buna we have been using.

This will aid in the sealing of the joint. We will also apply a filler of sawdust so that the paint will adhere to the repair. Press sawdust into the joint with your finger. Now you have a firm and invisible joint.

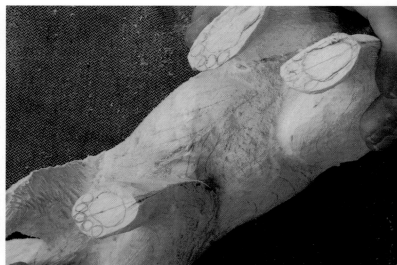

If you discover a seam or joint that has not sealed properly, like this one, you'll need to repair it. I'll show you how.

The joint is sealed. Allow the glue to dry for about an hour before working in that area.

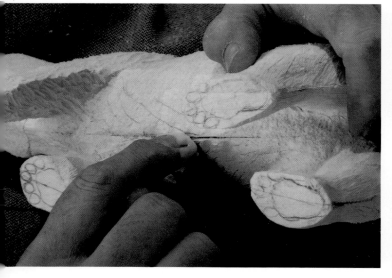

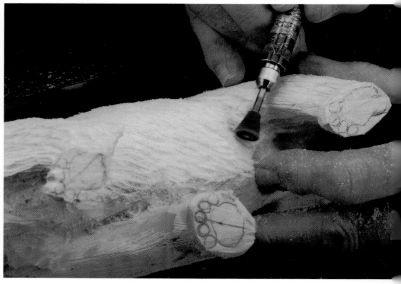

Take yellow carpenter's glue and force it into the seam with the tip of your finger.

Continue carving hair masses down the sides of the bear.

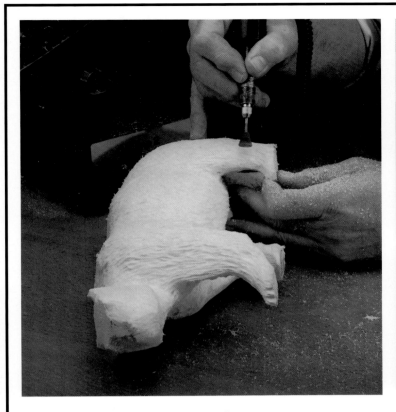

Continue down over the flanks as well.

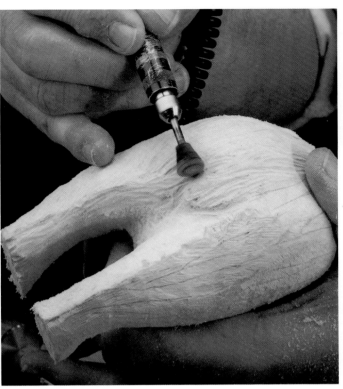

Make sure that the hair appears to come from underneath the polar bear's tail. By positioning your cutter at an almost flat angle to the body of the bear, you are able to give the hair around the tail the proper appearance.

Shape the toes on the rear feet in the same way you shaped the front toes.

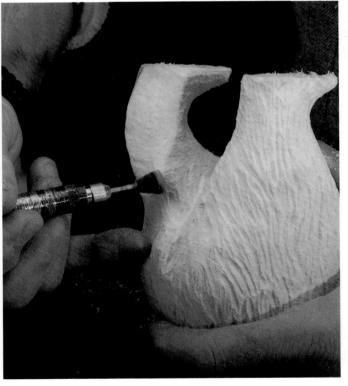

Make sure that the hair between the rear legs flows naturally down them. Always cut in the direction the hair flows or it will look wrong.

Here's the body with the hair cut in on one side.

The other side and the rear are now finished.

If your Kutzall burr has become clogged with glue, there are two ways to clean it. You may use either a copper wire brush or a propane torch to remove the sticky debris. The torch will not damage the carbide tips of the Kutzall burrs.

Sculpt the inside of the ear before carving away the too much behind the ear. This will prevent it from becoming too thin.

Change to a small cylinder Kutzall burr to cut in the hair on the face and the head.

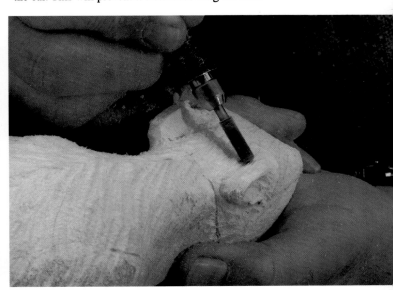

Shape the back of each ear.

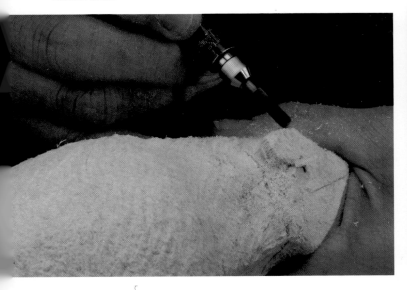

Shape in around the ears by holding the burr at about a 45 degree angle from your work.

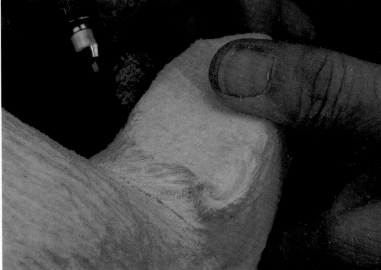

Pull the hair from the neck up onto the jaw, leaving it very heavy and course to indicate a ruff at the jaw line.

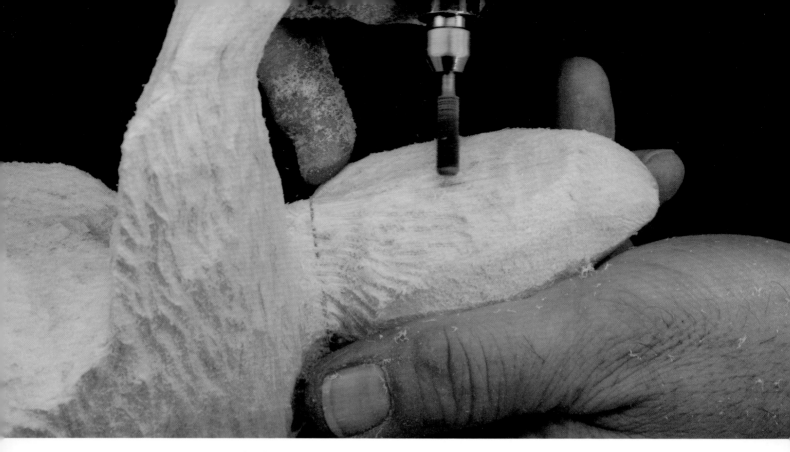

Cut the rough hair in on the neck and underneath the bottom jaw with very course cuts.

As you work toward the face, indicate hair on that face with very short, fine cuts.

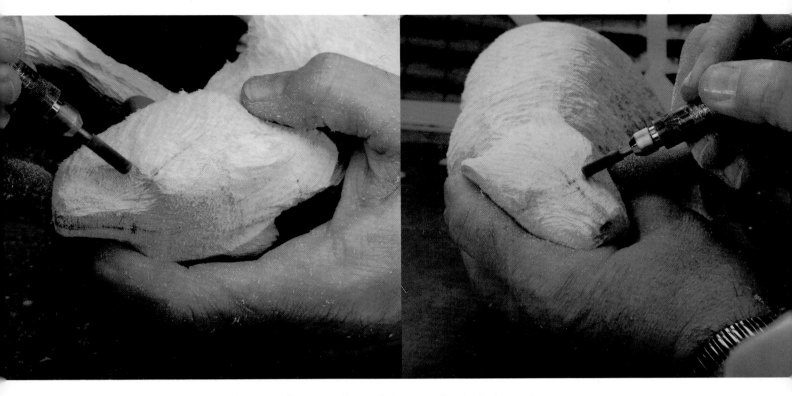

The cuts continue to get finer and closer together the farther up the
face you work.

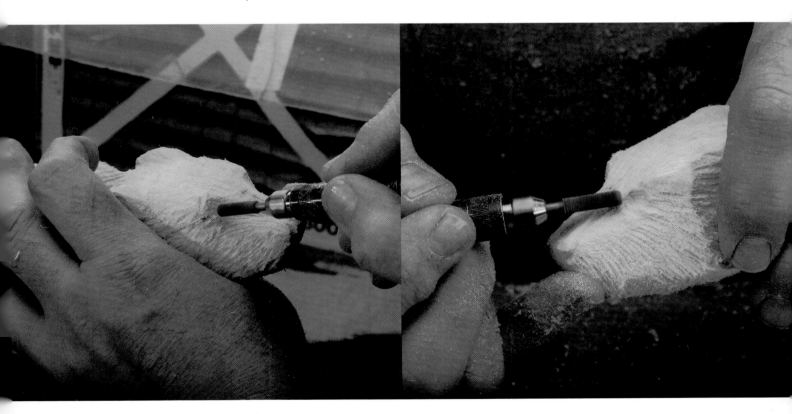

When preparing the surfaces into which the eyes will later be carved
and burned, make sure they are as straight up and down as possible.
Do not allow the eye surfaces to slope out at the bottom.

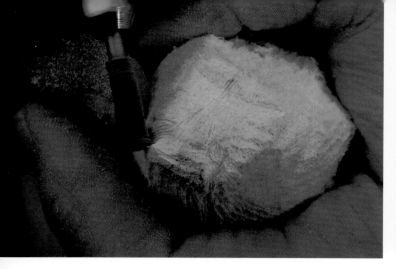

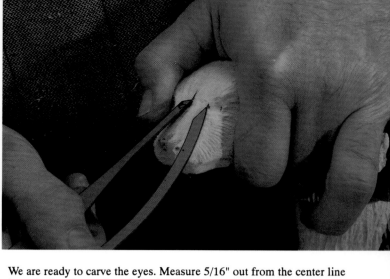

Start sculpturing the nose by cutting the areas where the nostrils would be. Cut the side of the muzzle away, allowing the nose to appear to stand out from the face.

We are ready to carve the eyes. Measure 5/16" out from the center line in each direction and mark the inside corners of the eyes.

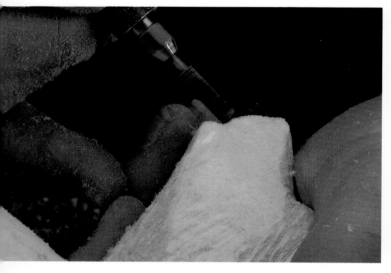

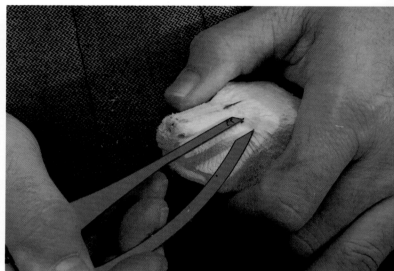

To shape the mouth, start by cutting a groove for the polar bear's mouth. Allow the bear's mouth to dip down in the back, giving him an almost unhappy, frowning look.

Measure 3/16" from the inside corner to find the outside corner of the eye. That gives you the size of the polar bear's very small eyes.

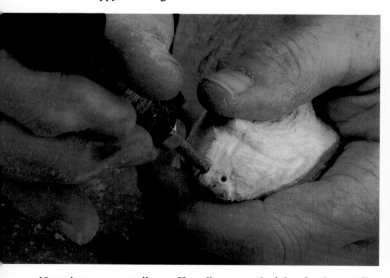

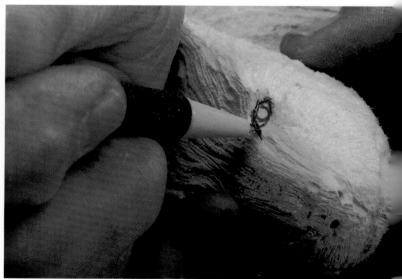

Now change to a small cone Kutzall to carve the inlets for the nostrils. The holes slope up slightly.

Measure and draw in both eyes.

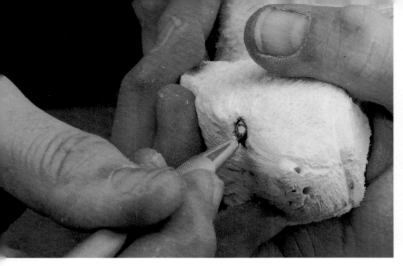

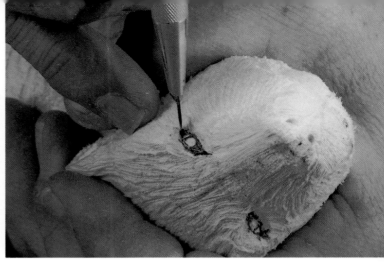

To carve the eyes in, we are going to remove two small, roughly triangular areas in the corners of each eye to define the eyeballs. First place a small blade into the inside corner along the bottom eyelid, with the point of the knife pressing into the eyeball

You now have an eye with a shaped eyeball.

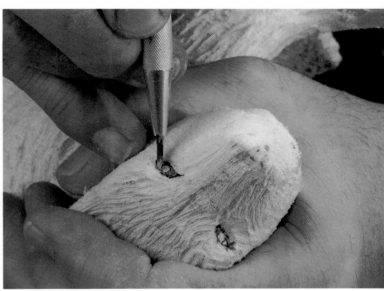

The second cut follows the upper lid with the point of the knife in the corner of the eye and pressing toward the eyeball.

Place the tip of your knife blade along the upper edge of the drawn in eyeball. Press it in at an upward angle to indicate that the eyelid protrudes out over the eyeball. Repeat this process on the bottom.

For the third cut, the blade is placed along the edge of the eyeball, resting the tip of the knife on the bottom lid. The blade is held at a slight angle along the eyeball and pressed in toward the inside corner. This causes a small, triangular chip to be cut out and the eyeball starts to appear. Repeat the same process on the outside corner of the eye.

Here are the finished eyes prior to burning.

We are now ready to begin burning in the polar bear's eyes with a wood burning tool. Polar bear eyes are quite small and must be burned with a small wood burning tip.

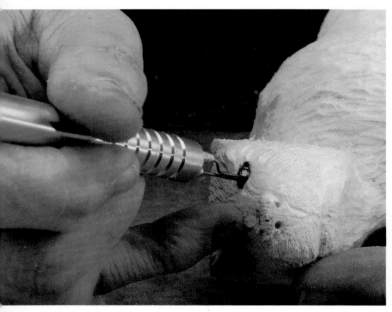

The first part of this wood burning technique uses the burning tip just like a knife. Start at the upper edge and draw the hot tip in toward the eyeball. Repeat on the lower line of the eye.

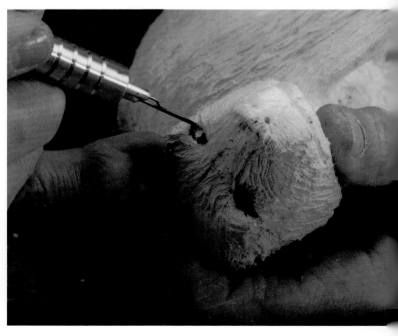

Repeat this process along the outside edge of the eye.

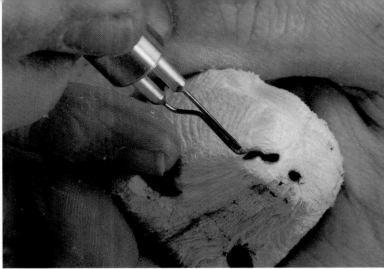

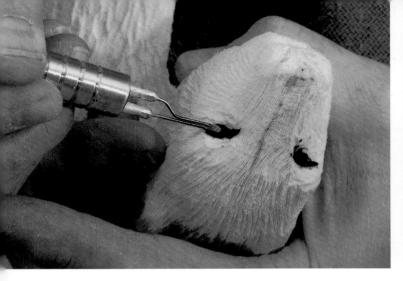

With the flat side of the burning tool, darken the eyeball itself prior to painting.

Burning the lines in on either side of the nose up toward the rest of the face.

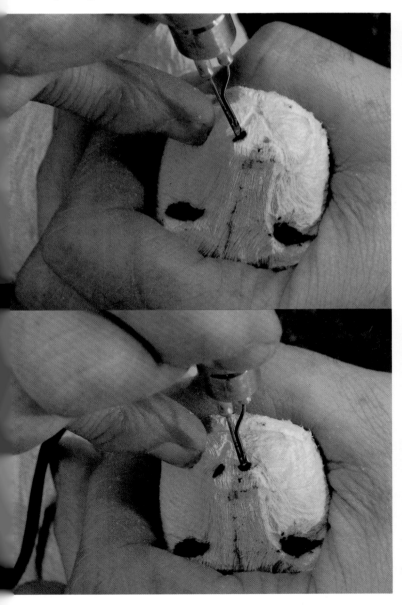

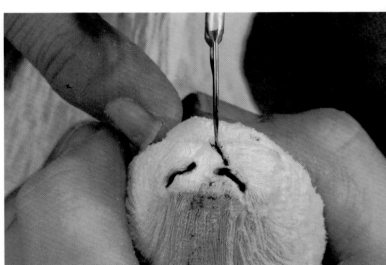

Indicate where the nose runs down toward the lips.

With your wood burner, darken the inside of the nostrils.

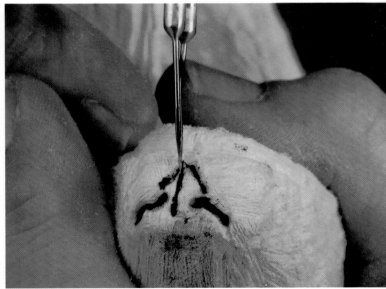

Burn in the center line on the nose.

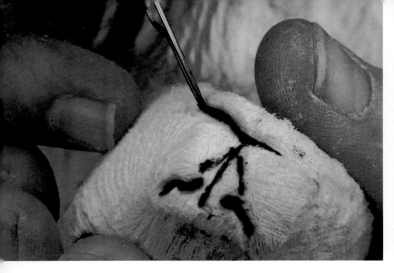

Burn in the lips. A polar bear's black skin shows on the lips and nose.

Here is the polar bear's face after wood burning.

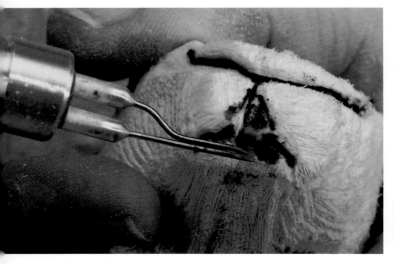

Darken the nose.

A polar bear's toe nails barely show at the furry tips of his toes. Indicate the toe nails with two small vertical lines put in on the end of each toe with the wood burner.

Now we need to lightly sand the bear by hand with 150 grit sandpaper. This removes the fuzziness left by the power tools and smooths off the tops of the hair so that there are no sharp corners when you run your hands over the bear.

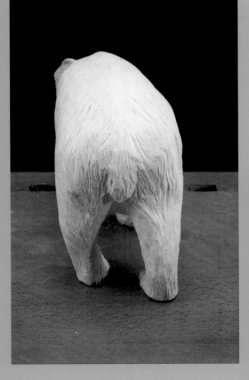

Now the polar bear is ready to paint.

Painting the Bear

In painting the polar bear there are only three colors you will use: white, dark ocher (yellow) and black. Begin with a very thin watered down wash of white. Apply with the grain, do not scrub back and forth. Back and forth motion causes the grain to rise, creating painting problems later.

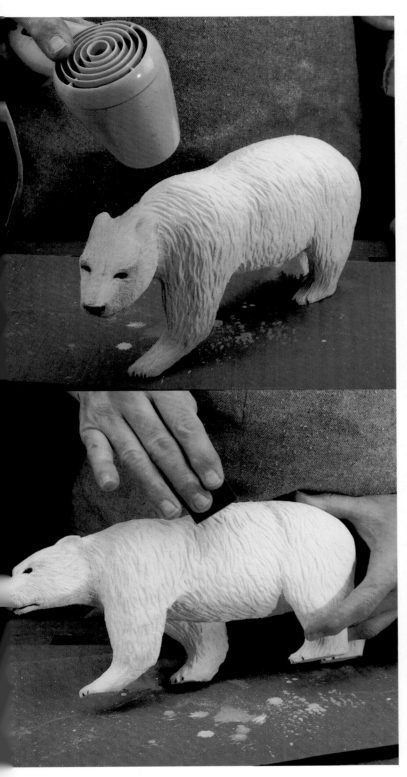

Use a hair drier to dry the wash; use the sandpaper to remove the small particles of grain that stood up because of the moisture in the paint. Sand in with the direction of the grain.

When you have finished sanding, put on a second coat of pure white-- barely diluted.

Mix a little bit of dark ocher and white to produce an off-color antique white. We're going to coat the bear with a very light coating of this mix, starting from his rump and working forward. This is a semi-dry brush technique (meaning you put paint on the brush and then wipe most of it out on paper before applying the paint left on the brush in a thin layer).

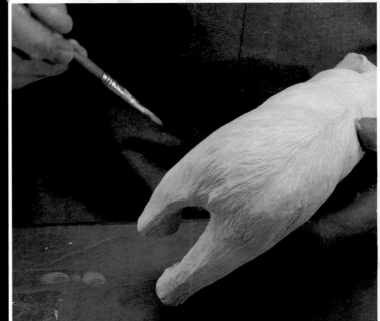

Here's the bear with the ocher applied.

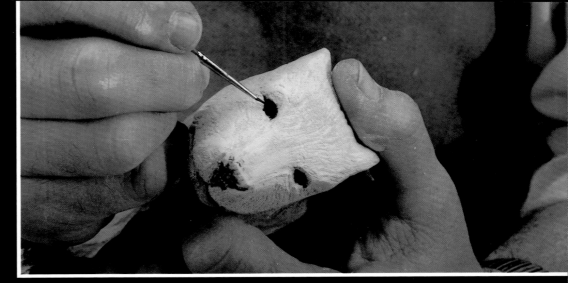

Paint the eyes black. Make sure that you cover both the eyeball and the exposed skin around the eye.

Cover the nose with black paint, making sure that all of the inside of the nostril is painted black.

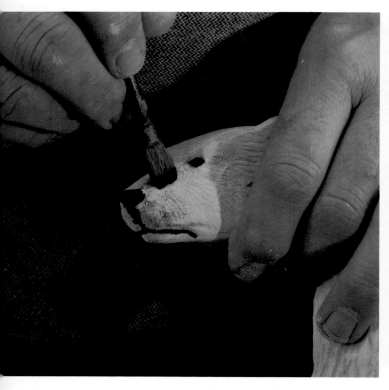

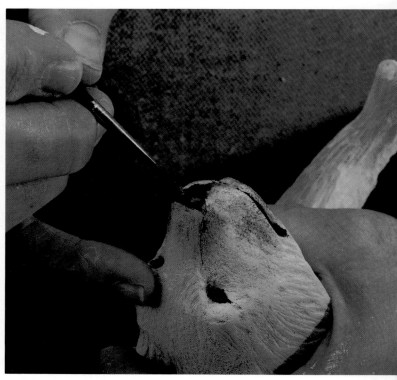

We're going to darken the bear's muzzle slightly. The hair is thinner there and the dark skin shows through. We will use the dry brush technique again, wiping the brush on a dry paper towel to remove most of the paint before applying the brush to the muzzle.

Applying acrylic to the nose.

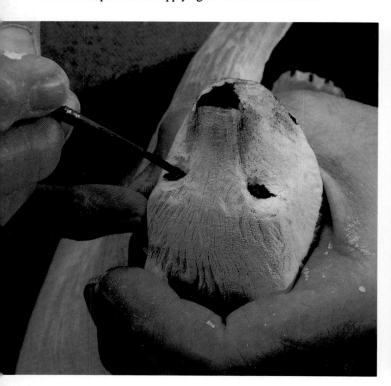

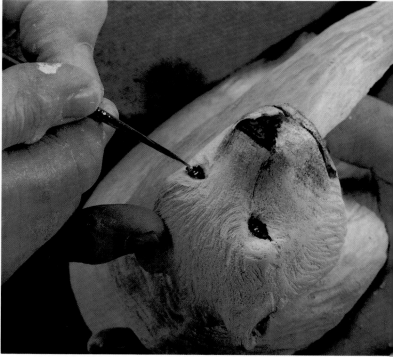

Put a clear acrylic gloss medium in the eyes and on the nose and lips to make them appear moist.

Add a white dot to both eyes to give them a little more life.

Your polar bear is finished.

The Gallery

Bear on a Stand

Enlarge pattern 118% for original size.

Black Bear Pattern (no model)

Hair direction
indicated by
arrows

Grain

*Enlarge pattern 120%
for original size.*